MW00657393

IMAGES of America

WORLD WAR II IN FORT PIERCE

This monument to Ft. Pierce's World War II activities is on the grounds of the Saint Lucie County Historical Museum on south Hutchinson Island. (Author's Collection.)

IMAGES
of America

WORLD WAR II IN FORT PIERCE

Robert A. Taylor

ARCADIA
PUBLISHING

ISBN 978-0-7385-0134-5

Published by Arcadia Publishing
Charleston, South Carolina

Printed in the United States of America

Library of Congress Catalog Card Number: 99-62807

For all general information contact Arcadia Publishing at:
Telephone 843-853-2070
Fax 843-853-0044
E-mail sales@arcadiapublishing.com
For customer service and orders:
Toll-Free 1-888-313-2665

Visit us on the Internet at www.arcadiapublishing.com

LCVPs (Landing Craft Vehicle, Personnel) maneuver off the coast of Ft. Pierce during a training exercise. (Saint Lucie County Historical Museum.)

CONTENTS

ACKNOWLEDGMENTS

The following individuals, institutions, and organizations made significant contributions to the creation of this book: Chief James Watson (USN-Retired), formerly of the UDT-SEAL Museum in Ft. Pierce; Edward Swanson, formerly of the St. Lucie County Historical Museum; Susan Kilmer of the St. Lucie County Library System; Edward Brisbois of the Amphibious Attack Boats-WW II Association; Ada Parrish of the Tebeau-Field Library of Florida History in Cocoa; and the U.S. Navy.

Special thanks go to Commander Louis J. Mullineaux (USNR) for service above and beyond the call of duty; William B. Thurston for sharing his memories; Dr. Nick Wynne of the Florida Historical Society for once again leading the way; George and Genny Taylor for putting up with another history project; Jim Taylor for lending a needed photograph; and lastly Virginia J. Dair for just being here. This book is dedicated to her, though the author retains all responsibility for all errors.

Robert A. Taylor
Ft. Pierce, Florida

INTRODUCTION

Few Florida communities were impacted by the Second World War as much as the town of Ft. Pierce. Its population soared along with its economy, and the small city made a large contribution to victory by hosting a major military training base. Located some 232 miles south of Jacksonville and 126 miles north of Miami, Ft. Pierce became a crossroads for thousands of servicemen and their families heading to the Sunshine State during the war years.

Military concerns played a role in Ft. Pierce's development from its earliest history. In the 1560s, Spanish conquistadors under Juan Valez Medrano established a small outpost along the Indian River at a spot they named Santa Lucia. This tiny bastion of Spain's New World empire proved in time untenable and was abandoned. Two centuries later, Spanish officials tried once more to claim the area by granting James Hutchinson some 2,000 acres of land for a plantation. This enterprise failed as well, though Hutchinson's name is still attached to the large barrier island separating the Indian River lagoon from the Atlantic.

War came to those same shores in 1835 as the Second Seminole War commenced on the Florida frontier. The U.S. Army faced a long and costly struggle against a determined enemy and needed bases along the coast from which to operate. In 1837, Colonel Benjamin K. Pierce, a veteran of the regular army, oversaw the construction of a small palmetto-log encampment on the bluff overlooking the river. Pierce, brother of the future president, named the fort after himself, and it became an active Seminole War post. Soldiers there, however, fought heat, insects, and boredom from behind Ft. Pierce's walls. Officers stationed there, like newly commissioned Lieutenant William Tecumseh Sherman, chafed at this less-than-thrilling duty but soldiered on as best they could.

When the Seminole War ground to a halt in 1842, Ft. Pierce was decommissioned, and the area reverted to a quiet wilderness. The new Armed Occupation Act, with its promise of free Florida land, sparked many to try settling near the old fort. Few prospered and fewer remained in the face of life on a very isolated frontier. By the late 19th century, steamboats and finally Henry Flagler's Florida East Coast Railroad (F.E.C) opened the area for true settlement. A growing population fueled calls for incorporating a city, which was done in 1901. Ft. Pierce now officially existed and soon became the seat of newly formed Saint Lucie County. World War I unfortunately brought hard times and contributed to the collapse of the local pineapple industry.

The Florida "boom" of the 1920s left its mark on the small city with big dreams. In 1921, dredges cut an inlet linking the Indian River with the Atlantic, thus making Ft. Pierce a port. A ship channel more than 3,000 feet long and some 27 feet deep, protected by limestone jetties, offered great economic promise. Soon, tons of citrus fruit, vegetables, and fish left regularly on ocean-going freighters after they unloaded general cargoes on the local dock. Sand from inlet dredging was dumped on what is now the southern half of Hutchinson Island to create a causeway, which is connected to the mainland by a toll bridge. A small beach resort known as "the Casino" lured bathers to the Atlantic beaches by this new route.

When the boom burst in 1927, the city by the river stood on relatively solid ground. Even during the Depression years the port remained active with ships from the Baltimore and Carolina Line docking regularly. The year 1934 saw the opening of a refrigerated warehouse on the docks that could handle all types of perishable products. The F.E.C. Railroad also served as an economic lifeline for cattle ranchers trying to get their beeves to market. All in all, the community weathered the depression of the 1930s and saw its population grow some 67 percent during that decade to over 8,000 people.

The bombing of Pearl Harbor ended Ft. Pierce's tropical idyll for the duration of WW II. A local serviceman died under Japanese bombs during that attack, which brought the war home to many local residents. Soon the war came closer as German submarines stalked targets off the south Florida coast, and locals volunteered to patrol lonely beaches at night watching for enemy activity. The U-boat threat severely limited the flow of shipping in and out of Ft. Pierce, dampening local commerce. The fortunes of war, however, would soon energize the sleepy cracker town.

The U.S. Navy learned from amphibious landings on Guadalcanal and in North Africa that it lacked enough properly trained small landing craft crews for successful operations. A new training facility to produce such sailors was desperately needed, and Florida seemed a likely location for it. A military survey team led by Captain Clarence Gulbranson (USN) looked at sites at St. Augustine and farther down the coast at Ft. Pierce. Gulbranson, a veteran of the North African landings, saw immediately the advantages Ft. Pierce had in the form of miles of empty coastline and easy access to the ocean through the inlet. Southern Hutchinson Island seemed ideal as a training site because it had almost no people, and the necessary utilities were already in place. Without consulting local leaders, the Navy picked Ft. Pierce as its newest Amphibious Training Base (ATB) and commissioned it as such on January 26, 1943.

The first soldiers and sailors to arrive had to hack out campsites on south Hutchinson Island with borrowed tools while setting up a training schedule with landing craft brought in from the Gulf Coast. In a few months, Ft. Pierce was a major military post with a national reputation. How these thousands of young men prepared for combat and lived under sunny Ft. Pierce skies is a story now ready to be told.

One

WAR COMES TO TOWN

When America entered the Second World War in December 1941, the nation underwent profound and permanent changes. Ft. Pierce, Florida, a small town on the Atlantic coast, was caught up in the conflict almost from the beginning as German U-boats plied the offshore waters hungry for targets. The year 1943, however, marked the community's major wartime transformation when the federal government moved to establish a U.S. Navy amphibious training base on Hutchinson Island along the ocean and banks of the Indian River. Soon, tens of thousands of sailors and soldiers came to this facility for amphibious and related education. By 1945, these military visitors would all but outnumber the townspeople in their own city.

Idyllic beach scenes such as these came to an abrupt end when Ft. Pierce shores were closed to civilian use by 1943. (Author's Collection.)

This is an aerial view of downtown Ft. Pierce, c. 1940, as seen from the Indian River looking westward. The yacht basin in the foreground would soon be filled with naval landing craft. (Author's Collection.)

Shown here is a pre-war view of Second Street in the heart of Ft. Pierce looking northward. (Ada Parrish Collection.)

The intersection of U.S. Highway 1 and Orange Avenue is depicted here as it appeared after WW II. The large structure in the center is the Mediterranean Revival-style Arcade Building, which housed military officers during the war years. (Author's Collection.)

Another Ft. Pierce landmark was the Raulerson Building, shown here, located on the corner of Second Street and Avenue A. (Ada Parrish Collection.)

By the 1940s, the impressive building of the Ft. Pierce Bank and Trust Company was about all that was left of the institution, as it failed during the banking crisis in Florida during the late 1920s. By the time of the war, locals and servicemen banked at the Saint Lucie County Bank, which enjoyed boom times due to thousands of new customers. (Ada Parrish Collection.)

Education in Ft. Pierce was centered at the Saint Lucie County High School on Delaware Avenue. It was built in 1914, in the Mediterranean Revival style, and today it is on the National Register of Historic Places. (Author's Collection.)

Ft. Pierce, being the county seat, boasted the Saint Lucie County Courthouse as a feature of the city in the 1940s. (Ada Parrish Collection.)

The city was fortunate to receive federal help during the Depression in the form of the construction of a new post office in 1935. It is located on Orange Avenue west of U.S. Highway 1. (Author's Collection.)

Survivors of merchant ships torpedoed by German U-boats in 1942 received treatment at the Ft. Pierce Memorial Hospital. Founded in 1937 by Dr. C.C. Benton and other prominent citizens, the hospital would soon feel the strain as the community grew during the 1940s. (Author's Collection.)

The Indian Hills Golf and Country Club, opened in 1941, was a local center for social life after the bombing of Pearl Harbor. By 1943, the club saw many public functions for military officers and their families and hosted such celebrities as golfer Gene Sarazen and boxer Gene Tunney. (Author's Collection.)

The "New" Ft. Pierce Hotel of the 1930s promised its guests a "delightful and inexpensive" stay along the shores of the Indian River. However, by 1942, the federal government would take it over for housing of the Coast Guard, Army, and Navy personnel for the duration of the war. (Ada Parrish Collection.)

Shown here is another view of the new Ft. Pierce Hotel looking eastward. Today, only the first section of the building still stands at the corner of South Indian River Drive and Atlantic Avenue. (Ada Parrish Collection.)

The Casa Caprona Apartments were first built north of Ft. Pierce in 1926 as part of the great Florida land boom of that era. All but abandoned when the boom collapsed, the building found new life as married officers quarters for those stationed at Amphibious Training Base-Ft. Pierce. Wartime residents included Lieutenant Commander Draper L. Kauffman, the founding father of the Navy's combat demolition "frogman" units. Today, the Casa Caprona is listed on the National Register of Historic Places. (Courtesy of Louis J. Mullineaux.)

When south Hutchinson Island became an amphibious training base in January 1943, the existing Coast Guard station became the new base headquarters. Built in 1937, the structure is at the present time Indian River Community College's Marine Science Center. (Courtesy of the U.S. Navy.)

The few private homes that existed on south Hutchinson Island were quickly commandeered for military use. The command car in the foreground wears the insignia of the Army's Fourth Service Command. (Courtesy of the U.S. Navy.)

Captain Clarence Gulbranson (USN) was the first and only commander of Amphibious Training Base-Ft. Pierce during the war. He was a 1912 graduate of the Naval Academy and a career naval officer. After serving as commodore of Transport Division One during the 1942 North African invasion, Gulbranson was assigned the task of creating a naval training center in Florida. (Courtesy of the U.S. Navy.)

Captain Gulbranson is seen here at his headquarters desk. During his tenure as base commander, he entertained important political leaders like Florida's Governor Spessard L. Holland as well as Senators Charles O. Andrews and Claude Pepper. (Courtesy of the U.S. Navy.)

The commanding officer conducts a formal inspection of naval personnel. Gulbranson was a stickler for military bearing and appearance, and woe was the sailor he found out of uniform or failing to render a proper military salute to a superior. (Courtesy of the U.S. Navy.)

On January 25, 1945, Captain Gulbranson received the Legion of Merit for his leadership and "exceptionally outstanding services" while in command at ATB-Ft. Pierce. Gulbranson rarely missed a day of duty despite poor health and the untimely death of his wife in 1944. (Courtesy of the U.S. Navy.)

Commander Perry M. Fenton was one of four ATB-Ft. Pierce executive officers to serve during the war. This 1922 Naval Academy graduate replaced Commander J.G. Farnsworth in August 1944 and remained at this assignment until September 1945. (Courtesy of the U.S. Navy.)

Commander Wilton S. Heald held the important post of officer in charge of all ATB-Ft. Pierce training activities from November 1944 to September 1945. He replaced Commander John C. Hammock. (Courtesy of the U.S. Navy.)

The U.S. Army trained thousands of soldiers in amphibious warfare at ATB-Ft. Pierce who went on to see much service in Europe and in the Pacific. In May 1943, Major Linwood Griffin Jr. became the senior Army instructor and is shown here seated at his desk in the Burston Hotel. (Courtesy of the U.S. Navy.)

In this photograph, an Army instructor works with trainees on stealth tactics and camouflage techniques on Hutchinson Island. (Courtesy of the U.S. Navy.)

Commanded by Lieutenant H.J. Hewitt Sr., one of the most active units stationed at Ft. Pierce was the Construction Battalion Detachment 1011. These "Sea Bees" lived up to their motto "Can do" on many base construction projects. (Courtesy of the U.S. Navy.)

This is a formal portrait of ATB-Ft. Pierce operations and maintenance staff. Seated in the front row, from left to right, are as follows: Lieutenant Commander B.M. Klivans, Lieutenant Commander R.E. Lindenmeyer, Lieutenant Colonel L. Griffin Jr., Commander P.M. Fenton, Captain C. Gulbranson, Commander C.V. Hatchette, Commander H.M. Matteson, Lieutenant Commander J. Kittele, and Lieutenant Commander K.D. Perkins. (Courtesy of the U.S. Navy.)

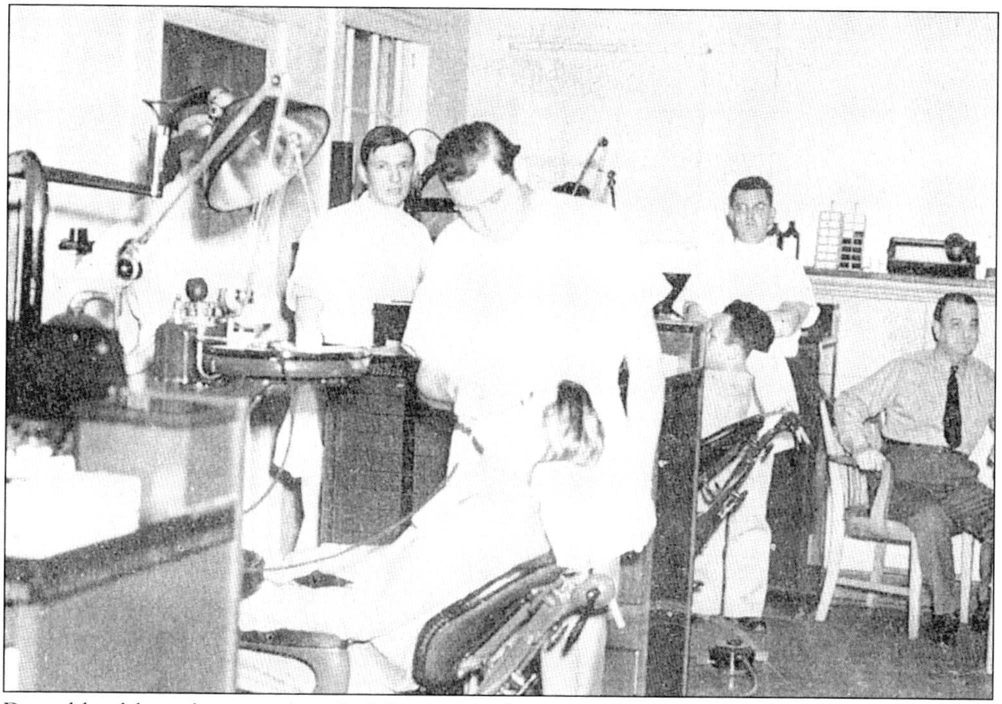

Dental health on base was handled day and night at a well-equipped dental office. The senior dental officer, Lieutenant Commander C.T. Miles, is shown seated at the desk on the right. (Courtesy of the U.S. Navy.)

One of ATB-Ft. Pierce's nerve centers was the base headquarters communication office. Seated at the teletype machine is Radioman E.M. Rzecyski, and standing from left to right are as follows: W.J. Hoag, F.H. Messer, M.T. Sharpe, F.X. Ricca, and C.B. Schutte. (Courtesy of the U.S. Navy.)

Many important visitors toured the Ft. Pierce base, inspecting training practices and equipment. This group, the National Inventors Council, arrived in February of 1945. The civilians on the front row, from left to right, are as follows: Dr. Roger Adams, University of Illinois; Dean Webster W. Jones, Carnegie Tech.; George W. Codrington, General Motors; Dr. Oliver

Buckley, Bell Telephone Laboratories; and John Green. In the vehicle, from left to right, are as follows: Oscar Ruebhowser; Walter Davis, Science Service; Dr. Charles F.K. Kettering, General Motors Research Corporation; and Dr. William D. Coolidge, General Electric. (Courtesy of the U.S. Navy.)

The Training Aids Office, located in the Attack Boat School area, was staffed by 2 officers and 11 enlisted men. The office, shown below, made and distributed over 90 different training devices from model ships to small bulkhead light blinkers. The Coast Guard station is in the background. (Courtesy of the U.S. Navy.)

An interior view of the Training Aids Office shows the projection and display room. (Courtesy of the U.S. Navy.)

Over 350 training films made up the base video library, with 145 being used on a regular basis. Nearly 14,000 trainees viewed such films each week as part of their preparation for active service. (Courtesy of the U.S. Navy.)

Shown here is the main gate entrance to ATB-Ft. Pierce on a typical day, looking eastward. Note the Amphibious Forces insignia on the sign in the center background. Today, the Saint Lucie

County Historical Museum is located to the left of the entrance. (Courtesy of the U.S. Navy.)

The vast majority of base trainees lived in these plywood and canvas tents that soon dotted the island. These "temporary" structures were the subject of much discussion among the men. (William B. Thurston Collection.)

Four officers pose for the camera before their tent/home in the spring of 1944. They are, from left to right, as follows: Ensign W.B. Thurston, Lieutenant (JG) William P. Fitzpatrick, Ensign P.J. Croak, and Ensign (?) Korwin. Ensigns Thurston and Croak would later see duty aboard the U.S.S. *Olympus*. (William B. Thurston Collection.)

These seven unidentified naval officers were assigned to the Amphibious Forces Attack Boat section and received training at Ft. Pierce in 1944. (William B. Thurston Collection.)

This is another view of the tents in Camp Number Two early in 1944. Note the white paint on the tree trunks to help make them visible after "lights out." (William B. Thurston Collection.)

Tenting on Hutchinson Island in the 1940s was no laughing matter. These shelters were hot in the summer, cold in the winter, and often infested with mosquitoes and sand fleas. (William B. Thurston Collection.)

Ensign (?) Bernays is shown here outside his tent in early 1944. Note the flap on the tent wall and the gravel path that ran through most of the island camps. (William B. Thurston Collection.)

Lieutenant (JG) William Fitzpatrick was a schoolteacher from the state of Washington before the war. After completing training in Ft. Pierce, he was assigned to an attack transport ship in the Pacific. Lieutenant Fitzpatrick was later killed during the landing at Lingayen Bay in the Philippines in January 1945. (William B. Thurston Collection.)

Recreation for men undergoing rugged training was essential for morale, and the Ft. Pierce community, both black and white, pitched in to help. Three USO clubs were organized on Second Street, Tenth Street, and Avenue D and staffed with local volunteers. These women were part of the Volunteer Service Organization who entertained servicemen at USO functions and brought a bit of home to these lonely men. (Courtesy of the U.S. Navy.)

This photograph depicts a typical dance at the Tenth Street USO Club. Many military men returned to Florida after the war and married local girls they met at such social gatherings. (Courtesy of the U.S. Navy.)

Motor Machinist's Mate Second Class Nick Dore "cuts a rug" with Leah P. Smith at the Tenth Street USO Club. (Courtesy of the U.S. Navy.)

When thousands of sailors and soldiers went to Ft. Pierce for "liberty," they were under the watchful eye of the Shore Patrol. They aided the small city police force in maintaining order and military discipline. Seated left to right are Lieutenant (JG) R.B. Johnson and Lieutenant (JG) Jack McGonagle. (Courtesy of the U.S. Navy.)

Base Personnel Congratulated

CITY OF FORT PIERCE
Fort Pierce, Florida
January 21, 1944

The Mock-Up Editor,
U.S.N. Amphibious Training Base
Fort Pierce, Florida

Dear Sir:

January 26th commemorated the first anniversary o the establishment of the U. S. Naval Amphibious Trainin Base at Fort Pierce. Little did we realize a year ago suc an important unit of our fighting force would become a par of our community. No one among us could visualize th achievements that have been accomplished by the men wh have had the responsibility of the undertaking. We do nc believe that any part of our preparedness for the great tas at hand has been prosecuted with more fervor or earnestnes than has been displayed by the men of your base. So it i with the greatest degree of pleasure I congratulate you Commanding Officer, Capt. C. Gulbranson, USN, and th entire Base personnel on a job so thoroughly done.

We of the community have been enriched by the man fine friendships established and although we will rejoice i the termination of present hostilities we hope that you wi be with us forever in memory if not in fact.

Again may I say congratulations on your first anniver sary and happy landings when you leave us.

Very sincerely yours,

D. O. McDougald
City Manager

This letter of praise from the Ft. Pierce city manager D.O. McDougald appeared in the ATB-Ft. Pierce base newspaper, *The Mock-Up*, in January of 1944. Relations between servicemen and townspeople remained generally good for the entire war with very few major incidents. (Courtesy of the U.S. Navy.)

Two

Scouts, Raiders, and Frogmen

The U.S. Navy Amphibious Training Base in Ft. Pierce soon became the school for some of the most elite units in the armed forces in the 1940s. The joint Army-Navy Scouts and Raiders program prepared American commandos for missions from the beaches of Sicily to far-off China. In 1943, the Navy set up its own demolition program at ATB-Ft. Pierce and hence the home of the legendary "frogmen." The training these young men received locally steeled them for the rigors of combat and contributed in no small way to eventual Allied victory.

Pictured here are Scout and Raider trainees drilling with LCRs (Landing Craft, Rubber) on the beaches of Hutchinson Island near Ft. Pierce. (Courtesy of the U.S. Navy.)

The Scouts and Raiders School was the first unit to commence operations at ATB-Ft. Pierce in January 1943. Shown here are some of the instructors of this program for elite commandos. From left to right are the following: (front row) Lieutenant W.P. McPherson, Lieutenant (JG) John J. Bell, and Lieutenant Frank McLean; (back row) Ensign R.F. Herrick, Lieutenant (JG) Max C. Peterson, and Ensign John R. Tripson. Bell, Herrick, and Tripson were holders of the Navy Cross for heroism in the 1942 invasion of North Africa. (Courtesy of the U.S. Navy.)

Intensive physical training was scheduled for all Raider and frogmen candidates. A day of rope climbing and pull-ups was not "a day at the beach" for these sailors and soldiers on Hutchinson Island. (Courtesy of the U.S. Navy.)

Rugged training with 400-pound logs, an idea borrowed from British commando schools, became a standard part of conditioning for Raiders and their Naval Combat Demolition counterparts. Such "log P.T." remains a staple of Navy SEAL training to this day. (Courtesy of the U.S. Navy.)

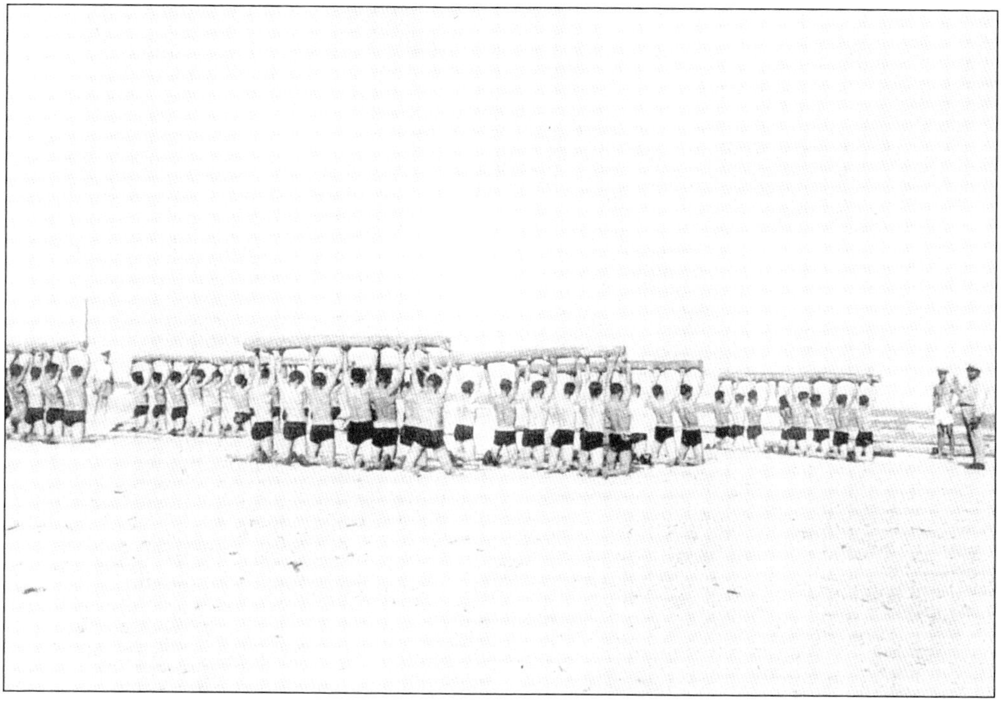

Clad in camouflage suits, two Scouts and Raiders School teachers return from a reconnaissance exercise. Ensign John R. Tripson (left) played football for Mississippi State and the Detroit Lions before the war. Captain George H. Bright (right) was a graduate of British commando training in Scotland. (Courtesy of the U.S. Navy.)

Raider trainees are shown in this photograph receiving a lecture on the various small arms they would use in combat. The officer/instructor is holding a .45 caliber M3 submachine gun, better known as a "grease gun." The building in the background was the Casino, a pre-war dance hall located south of the Ft. Pierce Inlet. (Courtesy of the U.S. Navy.)

This is a display of clothing, weapons, and equipment used by Scouts and Raiders in the field against the Axis forces. (Courtesy of the U.S. Navy.)

Rubber boat handling was essential to Scout and Raider operations, and pupils spent many hours mastering their maintenance and use. On any given day, the waters around Ft. Pierce abounded with these fragile crafts. (Courtesy of the U.S. Navy.)

Shown here is a "sea legs drill," as Raiders scramble down a cargo net into their rubber assault boats. One trainee painted his opinion of such activity on the bow of his boat. (Courtesy of the U.S. Navy.)

The main mission of the Scouts and Raiders was to gain information about enemy-held territory through amphibious reconnaissance. Here, Raider officer trainees learn photographic interpretation techniques. (Courtesy of the U.S. Navy.)

Raider officers and enlisted men pay close attention to a table display of an amphibious landing operation, the type their unit was meant to support. (Courtesy of the U.S. Navy.)

Hand-to-hand combat was a core subject during the 12-week Scout and Raider course, including jujitsu and effective ways to silence enemy sentries. (Courtesy of the U.S. Navy.)

Three Scout and Raider students, clad in camouflage coveralls and grease paint, stand ready for a scouting mission. (Courtesy of the U.S. Navy.)

Concealment was vital to Raiders infiltrating a hostile shore. In the above photograph, a trainee is about to hide among the flora on Hutchinson Island. By blending into the natural cover he becomes all but invisible to any observer, as seen below. (Courtesy of the U.S. Navy.)

In September 1943, the Second Ranger Battalion, commanded by Colonel James E. Rudder, attended the Scouts and Raiders School at ATB-Ft. Pierce to prepare themselves for amphibious operations. They later assaulted Normandy on D-Day, where elements of the Second Rangers assaulted the cliffs at Pointe Du Hoc. (James E. Taylor Collection.)

Soldiers paddle ashore during rubber boat drill at the Scouts and Raiders School. (Courtesy of the U.S. Navy.)

This photograph depicts a view of ATB-Ft. Pierce looking eastward toward the Atlantic. Raider and frogman training centered at the far seaward end of the island. The bay of water on the right was known as Faber Cove. (Courtesy of the U.S. Navy.)

The Naval Combat Demolition Unit (NCDU) program was established at ATB-Ft. Pierce in July 1943, to train men for the arduous task of removing beach obstacles set to impede Allied landings in Europe and the Pacific. Under the command of Lieutenant Commander Draper L. Kauffman, the soon-famous "frogmen" learned to handle explosives and rubber boats while enduring some of the toughest physical training the military could devise. Six-man teams ran and swam many miles in preparation for the rigors of combat. The above photograph shows Naval Combat Demolition headquarters as frogmen candidates form for morning muster. (Courtesy of the U.S. Navy.)

Frogmen trainees observe a class in rubber boat handling by NCDU instructors. Demolition men were expected to use these to make their way to the beaches, but later in the war they received considerably more training in long-distance swimming and shallow-water diving. (Courtesy of the U.S. Navy.)

A NCDU unit takes to the sea in their rubber assault craft. The standard uniform for frogmen trainees at Ft. Pierce consisted of steel helmets, combat fatigues, heavy boots, and life jackets. (Courtesy of the U.S. Navy.)

Basic seamanship, in the form of rope handling and knot making, formed an elementary part of all frogmen training. (Courtesy of the U.S. Navy.)

Demolition crews were expected to be familiar with all forms of naval communications, including the traditional flag hoist. (Courtesy of the U.S. Navy.)

Both future frogmen and Raiders were schooled in stealth tactics. Here trainees stalk a blindfolded man simulating night operations. (Courtesy of the U.S. Navy.)

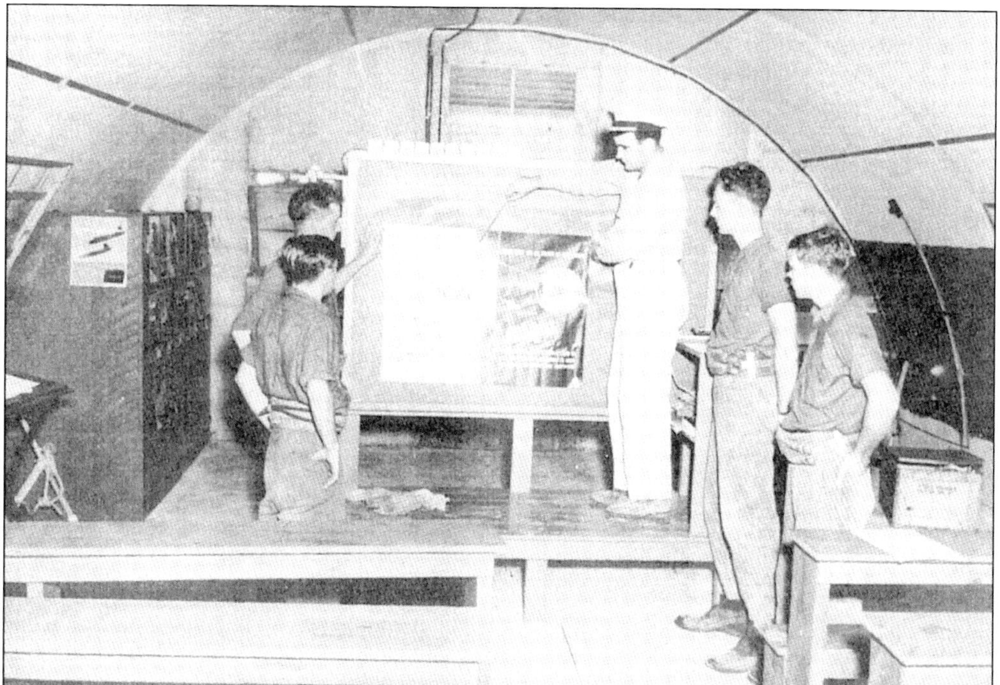

Frogmen trainees pay close attention to a lesson on the principles of night vision in a Quonset hut classroom. (Courtesy of the U.S. Navy.)

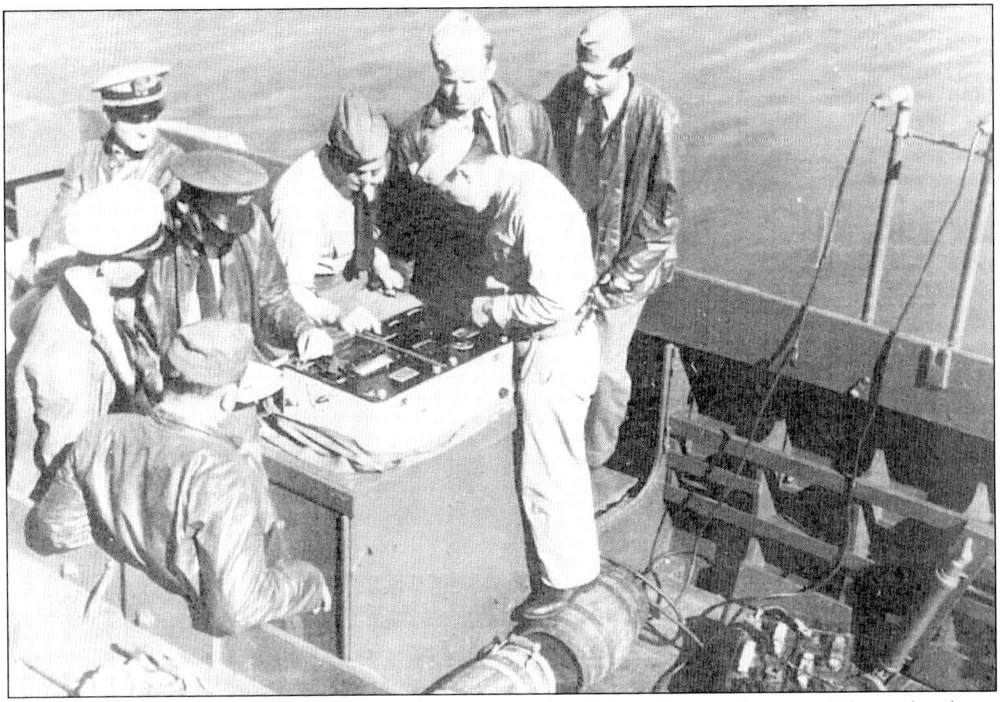

A key mission of frogmen teams was to chart the depths of shorelines before amphibious landings took place. Many combat swimmers painted black rings on their bodies in one-foot intervals and thus became human "rulers." Mechanical fathometers, such as the one being demonstrated above, made such measurements more precisely. (Courtesy of the U.S. Navy.)

Mine detection and removal occupied the men who were later assigned to UDTs (Underwater Demolition Teams). Here, sailors wrestle with shallow water mine sweeping gear on the stern of an LCVP. (Courtesy of the U.S. Navy.)

Shown here are "demolitioneers" loading a landing craft at Faber Cove for a short trip on the Indian River to north Hutchinson Island for a day of vigorous training. Note the rowboat "Sad Sack" moored in the foreground. (Courtesy of the U.S. Navy.)

Naval Combat Demolition trainees camp on north Hutchinson Island, north of the Ft. Pierce Inlet, while on a reconnaissance exercise. Today, this beach is part of the Ft. Pierce Inlet State Recreational Area. (Courtesy of the U.S. Navy.)

Since the frogmen's main mission was the destruction of German and Japanese beach obstacles to invasions, Construction Battalion Detachment 1011 spent over two years constructing such obstacles for demolition practice. The above photograph shows a steel "hedgehog" designed to hinder men and vehicles on a landing. This one and the others on the next page are on display at the UDT-SEAL Museum in Ft. Pierce. (Author's Collection.)

A "horned scully" made of cement and steel beams was designed to be planted on German-defended beaches below the waterline to wreck incoming landing craft. This one was among many removed from local waters in the 1990s. (Author's Collection).

This is another version of the "horned scully" with its wicked "teeth" set to rip the bottom of an LCVP "Higgins boat." (Author's Collection.)

"Bails" made of concrete, steel, or wood were placed at the high water mark to impede invasion craft. They were often tipped with high explosives set to blow on contact. (Author's Collection.)

Shown here are NCDU trainees at a rare moment of rest on top of a house located on the obstacle course. This 1944 photograph includes NCDU number 36, known as "Hamman's Sea Hawks." It consisted of Ensign Charles F. Hammon and enlisted sailors Sherman G. Prince, Henry Whitley, Gary J. Price, Raymond Royer, and Theodore G. Doerner. (Author's Collection.)

These frogmen are learning the proper use of the Mark 20 explosives pack. The pack contained a 2-pound block of C2 explosives and was meant to be quickly placed on an enemy beach obstacle. This practical device was developed by Lieutenant Carl Hagensen, and is still commonly known as the "Hagensen Pack." (Courtesy of the U.S. Navy.)

Student frogmen on north Hutchinson Island prepare lengths of hose packed with high explosives used in beach clearance. Wooden "bails" are shown in the background. (Courtesy of the U.S. Navy.)

This photograph depicts the plume from an 8,000-pound demolition charge on north Hutchinson Island. Blasts like these routinely rocked the citizens of Ft. Pierce around the clock and caused considerable damage to the city sewer system. (Courtesy of the U.S. Navy.)

Underwater breathing technology did not catch up to frogmen requirements until after 1945. Shallow-water diving equipment was crude at best and dangerous at worst. (Courtesy of the U.S. Navy.)

An underwater warrior models an early diving suit adapted for cold water missions. (Courtesy of the U.S. Navy.)

Trainees watch a diving instructor going over the side for a shallow diving lesson. Notice the cartridge belt pressed into service to weigh down the diver. (Courtesy of the U.S. Navy.)

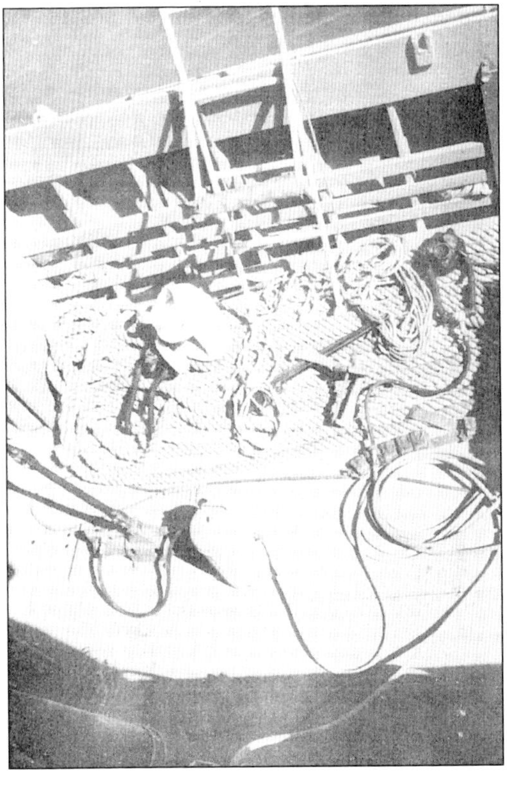

Shown here is a photograph looking down on the deck of an LCVP fitted out for shallow diving missions. At least one death was caused from the testing of new diving equipment in the waters off Ft. Pierce during the war. (Courtesy of the U.S. Navy.)

This statue shows a frogman-graduate of the Ft. Pierce school as he would have looked as part of a UDT in the Pacific. These "naked warriors" became legends in that theater and insured the success of many American landings there. This figure is on display at the UDT-SEAL Museum in Ft. Pierce. (Author's Collection.)

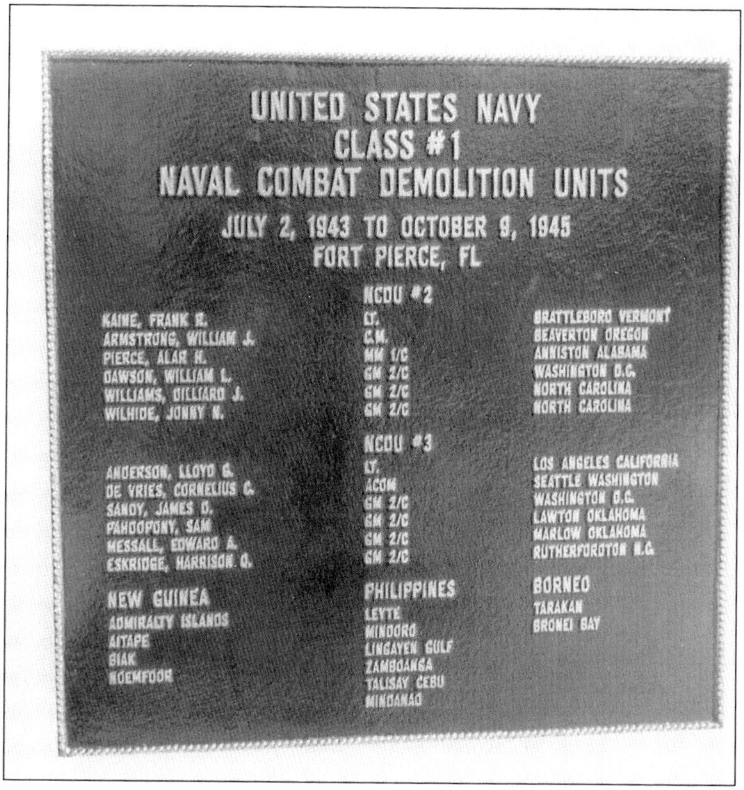

This is a memorial marker for the first NCDU graduating class from Ft. Pierce, a unit that saw active service in New Guinea, the Philippines, and Borneo. This and other team markers can be viewed at the UDT-SEAL Museum. (Author's Collection.)

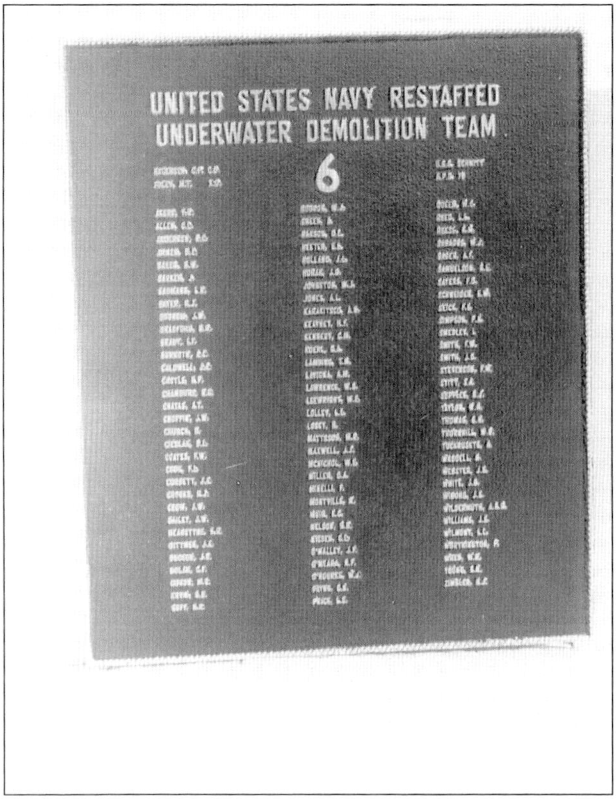

UDT Number Six completed four successful beach reconnaissance and clearing missions, often under direct Japanese fire, in the central Pacific by 1944. (Author's Collection.)

On November 9, 1986, this plaque was placed at the UDT-SEAL Museum on north Hutchinson Island, Ft. Pierce, Florida, in memory of all Raiders, frogmen, and their SEAL descendants who gave their lives in the service of their country. (Author's Collection.)

Three

Away All Boats

The main reason sleepy Ft. Pierce was converted into a bustling wartime training site was to produce expert small landing craft crews necessary for the amphibious assaults to be conducted in Europe and in the Pacific. These attack boat sailors, many of whom had never handled a boat or in some cases even seen an ocean, had to master the operations and maneuvering of such boats in all types of seas and under enemy fire. Army troops needed instruction in embarking and debarking from such crafts under simulated combat conditions. By 1945, tens of thousands of GIs and "swabbies" had completed the ATB-Ft. Pierce course and went on to gallant service overseas.

Troops climb down cargo nets into LCVP landing craft as part of attack boat training at ATB-Ft. Pierce. This training "mock up" was located on the south side of the Ft. Pierce Inlet. (Courtesy of the U.S. Navy.)

Sailors training on landing craft, or attack boats, passed through a specialized school in 531-man "floats" every eight weeks. The Attack Boat School was the largest of the schools at ATB-Ft. Pierce and is shown in the above photograph. (Courtesy of the U.S. Navy.)

The auditorium of Gulbranson Hall, opened in May 1944, often served as a classroom for attack boat trainees. It had a seating capacity of over 1,000. (Courtesy of the U.S. Navy.)

An engineering instructor gives landing craft sailors a lecture from the stage of Gulbranson Hall on the proper use of the standard issue fire extinguisher. Note the Amphibious Forces gold and scarlet insignia displayed on the walls. (Courtesy of the U.S. Navy.)

Sailors pay rapt attention to a training film on chemical warfare being screened in Gulbranson Hall. Allied commanders feared that desperate Germans or Japanese might use poisonous gas to stop amphibious invasions. (Courtesy of the U.S. Navy.)

Officers are shown here in a class on nautical navigation in the Attack Boat School. Most Amphibious Forces officers were naval reserve "90-day wonders" and needed as much professional education as possible. (Courtesy of the U.S. Navy.)

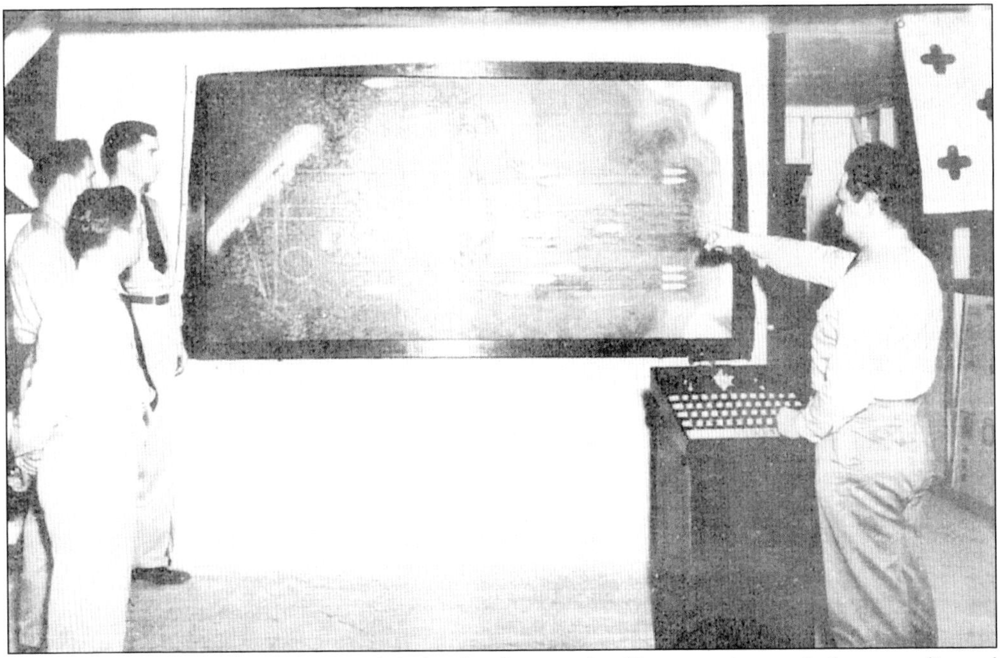

An electronic demonstration panel helps landing craft officers understand the complicated movements of an invasion force sailing from attack transport areas to the actual landing beaches. (Courtesy of the U.S. Navy.)

LCVPs were powered by 225 horsepower Gray diesel or 259 horsepower Hall-Scott gasoline engines. Here, crewmen train on actual engines in order to master their operation and maintenance. (Courtesy of the U.S. Navy.)

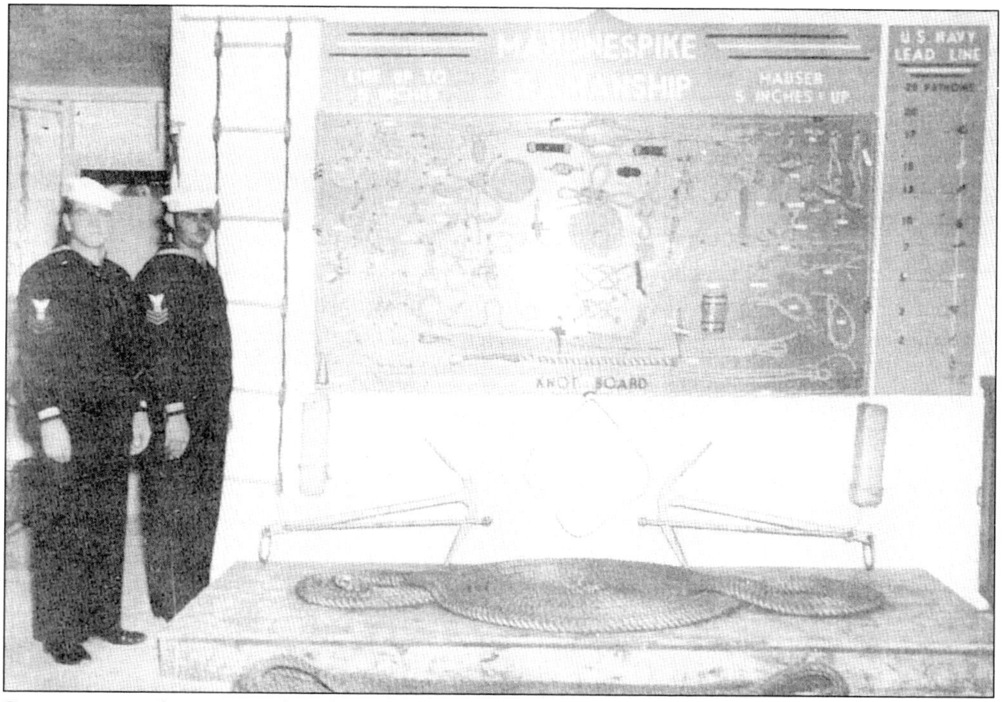

Since many sailors assigned to the Amphibious Forces had never so much as handled a rowboat, special emphasis on subjects like "marlinspike seamanship" was the order of the day in the Attack Boat School. (Courtesy of the U.S. Navy.)

Communications were vital to the success of all amphibious operations. Here, students at the Central Radio School train in sending and receiving Morse code messages. (Courtesy of the U.S. Navy.)

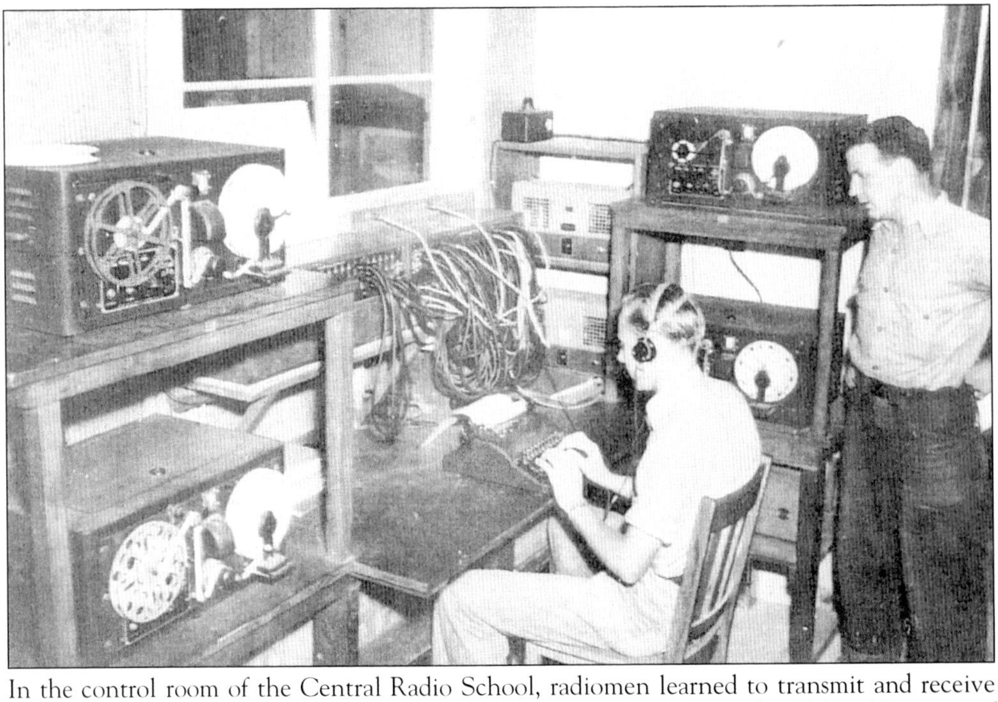

In the control room of the Central Radio School, radiomen learned to transmit and receive coded and "straight" messages. This was state-of-the-art equipment in the 1940s. (Courtesy of the U.S. Navy.)

Simulated "signal bridges" taught sailors flag communication as a part of the Attack Boat School training program. (Courtesy of the U.S. Navy.)

Sending and receiving messages by "blinker" light kept future signalmen busy as part of their training. (Courtesy of the U.S. Navy.)

Many landing crafts were armed with one or more machine guns. Gunner's Mates learned their weapons from these mounts and the stripping tables in the background. (Courtesy of the U.S. Navy.)

In an indoor classroom, sailors became familiar with various types of weapons they might use in action. In the foreground, there is a .30 caliber machine gun and a Browning Automatic Rifle, or BAR. (Courtesy of the U.S. Navy.)

A Special Weapons Unit instructor
traps in a Chemical Warfare buildin

These sailors/students master the i
Note the airplane models hanging fr

Shown here is a view of the Attack Boat camp on south Hutchinson Island. Note the numerous Higgins boat landing crafts moored at the docks or beaches on the inlet shore as well as the canvas tents that housed trainees. (Courtesy of the U.S. Navy.)

Instructional aids like this 15-foot scale model of an attack transport taught amphibious sailors rigging, cargo handling, and the proper storage of landing craft aboard. (Courtesy of the U.S. Navy.)

Ship models helped crews to visualize how landing craft were fitted aboard the larger troop transports. This particular scale model survived the closing of ATB-Ft. Pierce at war's end and is on display in the Saint Lucie County Historical Museum. (Courtesy of the U.S. Navy.)

Both landing craft crews and Army personnel learned the difficult task of loading troops from lowered cargo nets at this "mock up," located near the Ft. Pierce Inlet. Such realistic training paid real dividends during actual invasions. (Courtesy of the U.S. Navy.)

In time, the "mock up" was upgraded to include Welin davits, the type installed on attack transport ships. These gave crews hands-on training with the same model equipment they would be using at sea. (Courtesy of the U.S. Navy.)

Landing craft are shown here coming alongside the "mock up" for raising and lowering just as they would with actual troop transports. Its location made it convenient for access to the ocean through the Ft. Pierce Inlet. (Courtesy of the U.S. Navy.)

Army troops practice embarking with full field equipment into a landing craft. Note that these soldiers are still armed with the Model 1903 "Springfield" rifle and not the more modern M1 Garand. (Courtesy of the U.S. Navy.)

Troops are wading ashore on the beach of south Hutchinson Island. The LCVP on the right is in danger, and a salvage boat is coming to its aid. (Courtesy of the U.S. Navy.)

Trainees practice moving up and across open beaches with minimum exposure. These men would truly learn to love sand when under real enemy fire on a foreign shore. (Courtesy of the U.S. Navy.)

This photograph illustrates a view from the stern of an LCVP about to be hoisted up by fall lines at the "mock up." In the background is the entrance to the Ft. Pierce Inlet. (Courtesy of the U.S. Navy.)

A boatswain's mate mans the lines as an LCVP is lifted up on the Welin davit. The sign on the metal supports reads "no fishing from boat deck." (Courtesy of the U.S. Navy.)

All attack boat trainees received a few days training in landing craft other than the LCVPs. Among these were DUKW amphibious trucks, commonly known as "ducks." Here the staff of the ATB-Ft. Pierce DUKW School, Lieutenant J.A. Schwartza commanding, poses in front of their headquarters tent. (Courtesy of the U.S. Navy.)

Shown here is a DUKW turning amphibian with a crew of students aboard. This 2-1/2-ton vehicle could carry 25 soldiers and up to 5,000 pounds of cargo. (Courtesy of the U.S. Navy.)

Once underway, a DUKW could move at roughly 5.5 knots from its propeller and was steered by means of a rudder. This cruise probably took place on the Indian River lagoon. (Courtesy of the U.S. Navy.)

When back on dry land, the DUKW worked much like a truck with a top speed of 50 mph and a maximum range of 400 miles. This training "duck" sports neither the optional canvas cover over the cargo space nor the collapsible hood screen. (Courtesy of the U.S. Navy.)

Attack Boat School sailors also received operational instruction on the LVT (Landing Vehicle, Tracted). These "amtracs," or "alligators," were originally designed by Donald Roebling for use in the Florida Everglades and saw much service in the Pacific. This one is parked at the DUKW/LVT training area on the banks of the Indian River. (Courtesy of the U.S. Navy.)

Boat crew trainees receive instruction on an "alligator" before embarking on an exercise. The LVT could make 7 1/2 knots at sea and 20 miles per hour on land with its 250-horsepower engine. This power enabled it to crawl over obstacles such as coral reefs during landings. (Courtesy of the U.S. Navy.)

This photograph shows an LVT "alligator" entering the Indian River. The standard crew was four men, and the vehicle could carry some 4,500 pounds over 60 miles of open water. (Courtesy of the U.S. Navy.)

Attack boat crews were expected to be able to maneuver an LCVP alongside an "alligator" in order to transfer men and supplies for the run to an invasion beach or to take out the wounded. LVTs like this one were highly prized by amphibious forces island-hopping in the Pacific. (Courtesy of the U.S. Navy.)

An important adjunct to the Attack Boat School was the Beach Party program. A beach "party" consisted of 3 officers and 43 men and, with 8 other such groups, composed a naval beach battalion of some 450. Their vital mission was to mark beaches, direct landings, handle communication, make emergency boat repairs, care for and evacuate the wounded, and defend the beach area. Ten of the 12 beach battalions were trained at ATB-Ft. Pierce. Here, a trailer carrying a beachmaster's equipment is brought ashore by beach party sailors. (Courtesy of the U.S. Navy.)

An essential mission of the beach parties was to maintain steady communications along an invasion beach and with attack transports offshore. Flags, blinker lights, and public address systems all aided in these efforts, as seen here during training on Hutchinson Island. (Courtesy of the U.S. Navy.)

Palmetto plants give a Florida feel to this beach party's camouflage efforts. Each party had a communications section that served as a headquarters group. (Courtesy of the U.S. Navy.)

The operator of the 8-inch blinker searchlight blends in well with the surrounding plant life. Behind him sailors dig-in to position the light's generator. (Courtesy of the U.S. Navy.)

Radiomen practice entrenching themselves and their equipment under simulated combat conditions. These men had to constantly keep on the alert for any poisonous snakes that they might disturb. (Courtesy of the U.S. Navy.)

An officer-instructor supervises the assembly of radio equipment in a foxhole. These sailors probably never dreamed they would be digging foxholes while in the Navy. (Courtesy of the U.S. Navy.)

A radioman passes a message to a runner from his inland position on the landing beach. Beach parties could almost always count on coming under enemy fire while carrying out their missions. (Courtesy of the U.S. Navy.)

A beach party's hydrographic section mans a bowline to stop the LCVP they are unloading from being "broached" by the incoming waves. The sailor on the left is hauling a box of ammunition onto the beach. Such landing exercises were conducted as close to actual operations as possible. (Courtesy of the U.S. Navy.)

Beach parties and their parent beach battalions had to care for the expected flow of casualties on an invasion beach. All hands received training in basic first aid and the proper handling of the wounded. These sailors are learning how to move a stretcher case. (Courtesy of the U.S. Navy.)

The locations of body pressure points that control bleeding are explained with a smiling, simulated battle casualty. None of these men would find such work amusing under actual battle conditions. (Courtesy of the U.S. Navy.)

Another simulated casualty is carried through the sand to prepare these hospital apprentices for evacuating real wounded. The Atlantic can be seen in the background as these sailors trudge northward on Hutchinson Island. (Courtesy of the U.S. Navy.)

A medical officer instructs beach party men on the use of lifesaving plasma at a temporary aid station dug in the sand. Among their other duties, the Sixth and Seventh Beach Battalions, both trained at ATB-Ft. Pierce, tended real wounded on Omaha Beach. (Courtesy of the U.S. Navy.)

Beach battalions were expected to defend themselves and their beachheads from any enemy counter-attack. All members received instruction in the use of small arms and rudimentary combat tactics. Here, a gunner's mate shows the proper way to strip a Thompson .45 caliber sub-machine gun for cleaning. (Courtesy of the U.S. Navy.)

Beach battalion sailors faced daily weapons inspections to teach the vital importance of well-cleaned firearms. The man in the foreground holds his .30 caliber M1 Carbine ready for the inspector's critical eye. (Courtesy of the U.S. Navy.)

Each beach party had a boat repair section ready to make emergency overhauls of landing craft. Here an engineering officer explains the workings of a Gray marine diesel engine. (Courtesy of the U.S. Navy.)

Boat repair trainees install a marine engine on a LCVP with the help of a LeTourneau crane. An engine failure on a boat during an actual landing could have serious consequences, and all efforts were made to keep them in good working order. (Courtesy of the U.S. Navy.)

Shown here is an interior view of the cargo deck and engine compartment of an LCVP. This craft is on permanent display on the grounds of the St. Lucie County Historical Museum. (Author's Collection.)

This is a view of the bow section of the same LCVP. Its heavy metal ramp is deployed as it would have been when unloading on a beach. Thousands of these wooden boats were produced during WW II, but only a scant few remain today. (Author's Collection.)

This LCVP rests peacefully only a few yards from the Indian River, where hundreds once sailed. The symbol on its bow is that of the U.S. Navy Amphibious Forces of the Second World War. (Author's Collection.)

For tens of thousands of sailors and soldiers who were trained at ATB-Ft. Pierce, this is how they will remember the LCVP. The lowly "Higgins boat" made a contribution to Allied victory far beyond its size or cost of construction. (Courtesy of the U.S. Navy.)

The Amphibious Attack Boats Association of WW II veterans erected this stone marker as a permanent reminder and memorial of the training that went on in Ft. Pierce between 1943 and 1945. Ironically, it is one of the few such monuments that remember Andrew Jackson Higgins (1886–1952), the boat's designer and builder. (Author's Collection.)

Four

SCHOOL FOR VICTORY

WW II created a serious demand for military men with a variety of skills. All over Florida, bases like ATB-Ft. Pierce taught these (at times) deadly occupations in support of the war effort. In classrooms, "mock ups," gunnery ranges, and at sea, sailors learned to man guns of all types, including new rocket batteries. These men were disciplined to be effective lookouts and to make use of night vision. Training helped take some of the terror out of facing possible Axis chemical attack while in action as well as teaching sailors to recycle precious landing craft for future missions. More than a few would use these skills in post-war civilian life to build both a new Florida and a new America.

Sailors are shown here being tested for night blindness with a Radium-Plaque Adaptometer. Some 700 men were tested each week at ATB-Ft. Pierce as part of the Night Lookout training program. (Courtesy of the U.S. Navy.)

LCS (L)s (Landing Craft Support, Large) were LCIs (Landing Craft Infantry) converted into gunboats to provide close-in fire support to invasion forces. LCS (L) crews received some eight weeks of training in gunnery, recognition, lookout skills, and the all-important seamanship. Here, trainees learn about the trigger mechanism of the 20mm Oerlikon anti-craft gun in the gunnery building. (Courtesy of the U.S. Navy.)

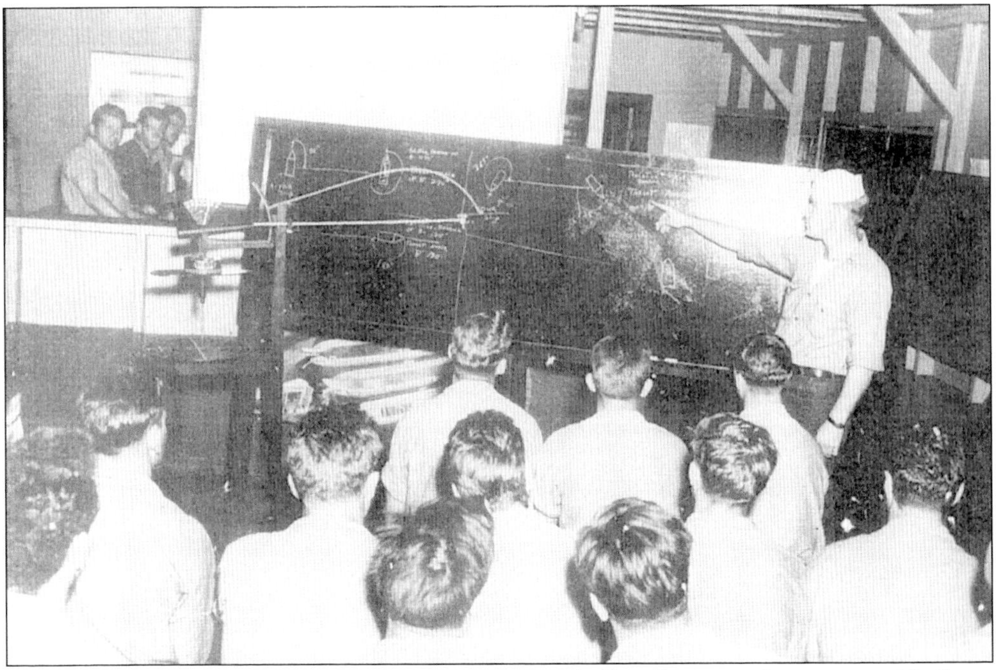

An instructor in the LCS (L) gunnery school uses "chalk talk" to explain a typical ballistic problem gunners would face in action. (Courtesy of the U.S. Navy.)

This Mirror Range Estimation Training Device helped teach apprentice gunners to quickly acquire targets through gunsights. Such training was invaluable under actual enemy fire. (Courtesy of the U.S. Navy.)

Sailors received hands-on training with the 20mm Oerlikon anti-aircraft gun on a special "dry" firing range at the LCS (L) School. This and the heavier 40mm gun were meant to defend against low-flying aircraft and dive-bombers. (Courtesy of the U.S. Navy.)

Shown here is a view of the LCS (L) "dry" firing gunnery range. The weapon in the foreground is a 40mm anti-aircraft gun. (Courtesy of the U.S. Navy.)

Here is a closer look at a 40mm gun crew drilling on the "dry" firing range. In combat, the two loaders were kept very busy feeding the weapon with 3-shell clips. (Courtesy of the U.S. Navy.)

LCS (L)s were equipped with the Mark 51 gun director and the Mark 14 gunsight. Both were used to direct fire from the craft's gun to enemy targets. Here, an instructor demonstrates its use to trainees. (Courtesy of the U.S. Navy.)

As always the LCS (L) training program stressed basic seamanship in the face of a large number of "land-lubber" trainees. Here future "salts" practice the age-old tradition of knot tying. (Courtesy of the U.S. Navy.)

Line handling was a basic part of the sailor's job. Here LCS (L) men practice the proper way to moor a ship to a dock. (Courtesy of the U.S. Navy.)

This photograph offers a closer view of the simulated main deck of a ship where sailors learned to use the heaving line and how to make fast all moving lines. A mistake with a line could cause major damage to a vessel, and such training was taken seriously. (Courtesy of the U.S. Navy.)

Another "mock up" used in LCS (L) training was a simulated signal bridge. Here, signalmen practiced visual communications such as semaphore and blinker lights. (Courtesy of the U.S. Navy.)

LCS (L) trainees are seen here putting messages together from the flag locker. Note the Amphibious Forces patch on the instructor's white jumper. (Courtesy of the U.S. Navy.)

LCS (L) gun crews eventually went to sea from Ft. Pierce for live fire exercises off south Hutchinson Island. Here, men prepare to fire a 3-inch naval gun at a target. For years after the war, spent shells washed up on local beaches as reminders of this activity. (Courtesy of the U.S. Navy.)

Fire! This 3-inch naval gun has just been discharged with smoke coming from the breech and a spent shell casing banging on the LCS (L) deck. Such gunfire helped soldiers and marines wade to shore on several hostile beaches. (Courtesy of the U.S. Navy.)

Here a 40mm anti-aircraft gun crew are target shooting from the same LCS (L) off Ft. Pierce. Note the signalman "talker" in the background and the ready ammunition attached to the sides of the gun "tub." (Courtesy of the U.S. Navy.)

During WW II, scientists developed rockets small enough to be fired in salvos from converted landing craft to pummel enemy beach defenses before landings actually began. LCS (L) crews, along with other attack boat sailors and beach parties, received instruction from the Central Rocket School. The above image is a cross-sectioned model of the standard 4.5-inch rocket. (Courtesy of the U.S. Navy.)

A pith-helmeted Rocket School instructor explains the design and function of the 4.5-inch rocket launcher. Twenty such launchers gave the modified rocket craft quite a punch. (Courtesy of the U.S. Navy.)

The Rocket School utilized a 105-foot LCT (Landing Craft Tank) to train sailors as proper rocketeers. Two launchers are set up forward on the LCTs well deck, complete with flash plates to contain the rocket's tail flame. (Courtesy of the U.S. Navy.)

LCS (L) trainees assembled 4.5-inch rockets on the deck of the Rocket School's LCT. Such a craft converted to rocket launching could hurl over 1,000 of these missiles at the enemy. (Courtesy of the U.S. Navy.)

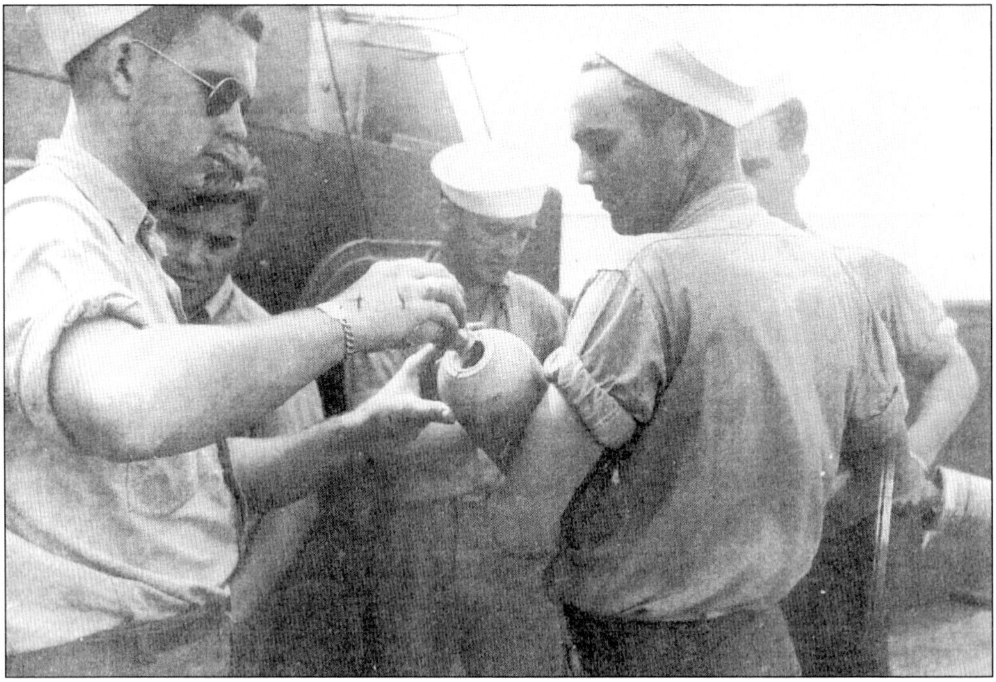

The detonating fuse had to be installed in every rocket before loading into a launcher rack. Arming each rocket in this manner required a steady hand and a cool temperament. (Courtesy of the U.S. Navy.)

Next, each armed rocket is gingerly loaded into its launcher. The safety pins are then removed, and the missiles are ready for firing electrically. (Courtesy of the U.S. Navy.)

These two launch racks of 4.5-inch rockets are ready for firing. LCS (L) trainees gained much practical experience with realistic hands-on training like this. (Courtesy of the U.S. Navy.)

The gunner's mate in charge selects the desired firing pattern then ignites the rockets from this control box. South Hutchinson Island routinely suffered the effects of these friendly missile barrages. (Courtesy of the U.S. Navy.)

By 1944, ATB-Ft. Pierce had its very own gunnery range on south Hutchinson Island, after having used the Ft. Pierce Police Department's target range. Weapons from .45 caliber pistols to 3-inch naval guns could be fired. Here, attack boat trainees fire Thompson sub-machine guns. (Courtesy of the U.S. Navy.)

Sailors are shown in this photograph firing the .45 caliber service automatic on the target range. Rifle targets are placed farther back along the top of the sand embankment. (Courtesy of the U.S. Navy.)

A young sailor receives help with the sights of a Springfield rifle on the firing line. Sailors and soldiers used outdated weapons for training in the United States due to shortages of M1 Garands. (Courtesy of the U.S. Navy.)

Shown here is another view of ATB-Ft. Pierce's rifle range. The Gunnery Training Department, consisting of 15 officers and 145 enlisted men, administered all weapons training on the base. (Courtesy of the U.S. Navy.)

These attack boat gunners are shown here waiting in line to fire .50 caliber machine guns at an aerial target. Planes from the naval air station in nearby Vero Beach towed target sleeves to sharpen their anti-aircraft skills. (Courtesy of the U.S. Navy.)

This image illustrates .50 caliber machine guns and 20mm anti-aircraft guns blazing away at towed airbourne targets. Note the sailor in the foreground with his fingers in his ears to protect his hearing from the noise. (Courtesy of the U.S. Navy.)

The Night Lookout and Night Vision Building helped evaluate and train thousands of sailors at ATB-Ft. Pierce in nocturnal recognition and gunnery. (Courtesy of the U.S. Navy.)

Sailors receive instruction in identifying ship silhouettes at the darkened Night Lookout training stage. (Courtesy of the U.S. Navy.)

Synthetic training devices like the Mark 1 Polaroid gunnery machine helped gun crews hone their skills without expending needed ammunition. Here, a class learns about proper tracer bullet control from an instructor. (Courtesy of the U.S. Navy.)

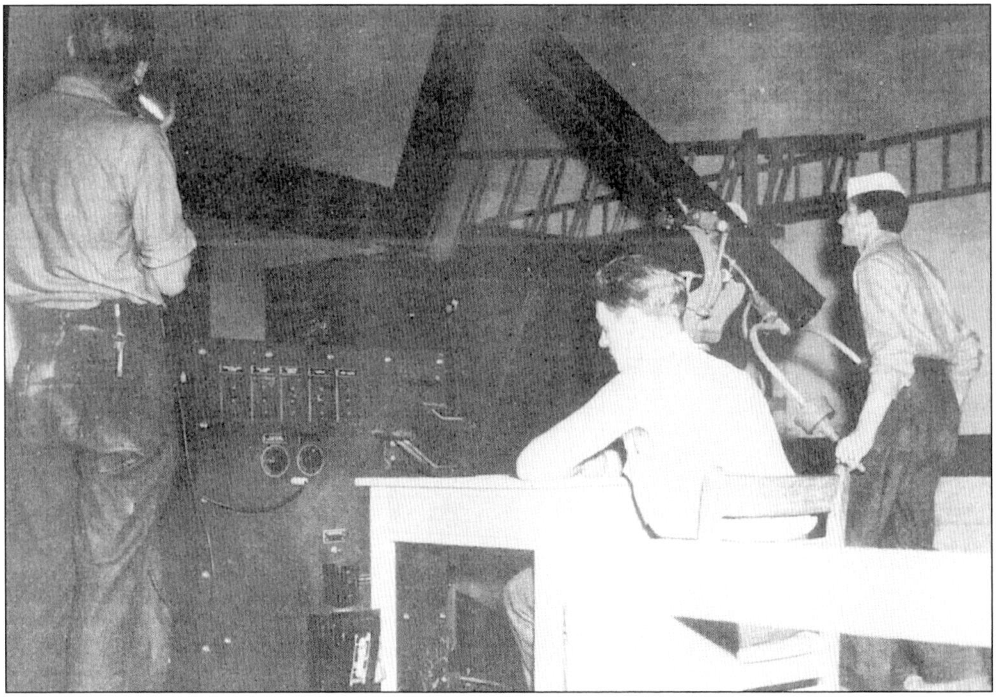

Shown here is a frontal view of the Mark 1 Polaroid trainer being used by a student gunner and the training staff. (Courtesy of the U.S. Navy.)

Under their instructor's watchful eyes, these novice gunners practice firing on the Mark IV Panoramic gunnery trainer. (Courtesy of the U.S. Navy.)

As with all ATB-Ft. Pierce training, classroom instruction received a significant emphasis. Here, gunners learn the intricate workings of the Mark 14 gunsight. (Courtesy of the U.S. Navy.)

A very serious subject for ATB-Ft. Pierce trainees was taught at the Central Chemical Warfare School. Students learned to identify chemical agents the Axis powers might use, protection from them, and decontamination procedures. This photograph shows a chemical warfare classroom with its visual aids. (Courtesy of the U.S. Navy.)

The Chemical Warfare School offered some nine hours of classroom and fieldwork training. Here a class sits in Gulbranson Hall watching a demonstration of a smoke pot used in camouflage. (Courtesy of the U.S. Navy.)

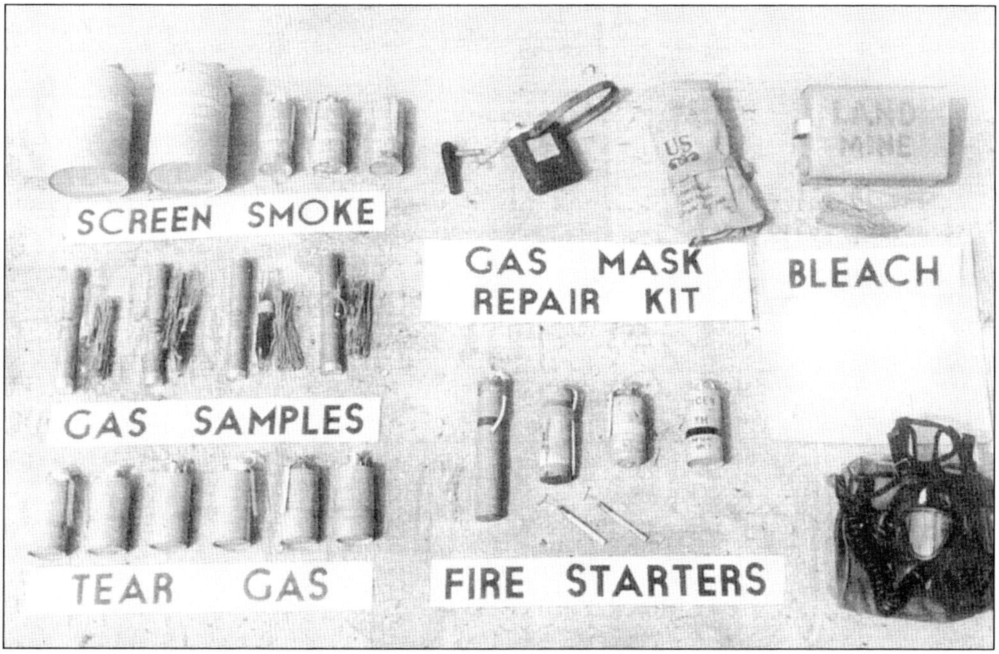

This is a display of equipment that was used in the fieldwork phase of chemical warfare training. All nations involved in WW II had the capacity to use such weapons, but they rarely did. (Courtesy of the U.S. Navy.)

A white phosphorous hand grenade explodes as part of a demonstration. Burns from such a weapon were horrible and difficult for medical personnel to treat. (Courtesy of the U.S. Navy.)

One of the six enlisted instructors at the Chemical Warfare School shows the proper use of an individual protection cover in the event of a poison gas attack. (Courtesy of the U.S. Navy.)

Once under the cover, the men would have time to don the standard issue Mark IV gas mask and continue their duties. Fortunately, American fighting men had no need to use these masks while under fire. (Courtesy of the U.S. Navy.)

Less than eager sailors draw gas masks prior to a drill using real chemical agents. (Courtesy of the U.S. Navy.)

From the platform the instructor takes students through a gas mask drill. Note the white "dixie cup" hats between each sailor's knees. (Courtesy of the U.S. Navy.)

Now clad in their masks, sailors learn to breathe through them. Such a drill was unpleasant when carried out under the Florida summer sun. (Courtesy of the U.S. Navy.)

Tear gas and chemical smoke are shown here being released among the trainees in the final part of the gas mask drill. Sailors were often ordered to remove their masks to get a taste of the tear gas and to learn not to panic. (Courtesy of the U.S. Navy.)

An officer looks on as a sailor in protective clothing uses a dry chemical mix to smother an incendiary bomb. Such exercises were included in chemical warfare training. (Courtesy of the U.S. Navy.)

Incendiary devices could also be rendered harmless with water. One sailor pumps water from a bucket while another sprays a weak stream of water. (Courtesy of the U.S. Navy.)

Because landing craft were so vital to Allied amphibious operations, ATB-Ft. Pierce boasted a Landing Craft Salvage School to train 18-man salvage crews to save and refurbish such boats. Here, salvage trainees grapple with an LCVP in danger of "broaching" along the beach. (Courtesy of the U.S. Navy.)

A salvage boat prepares to tow a beached LCVP out to sea as crewmen wade through the surf to make fast the towing cables. (Courtesy of the U.S. Navy.)

An LCM (Landing Craft Mechanized) converted for salvage work picks up the stern of an LCP (L) (Landing Craft, Personnel Large). The latter type is the original rampless model designed by Andrew J. Higgins. (Courtesy of the U.S. Navy.)

The LCMs marine engines were powerful enough to pull a landing craft off a beach and out beyond the surf for repairs. Ft. Pierce beaches provided excellent training grounds for such work. (Courtesy of the U.S. Navy.)

A LeTourneau crane lifts a 37-foot LCP (L) out of the water while a bulldozer prepares to haul it to a repair shop. This operation appears to have taken place along the Indian River. (Courtesy of the U.S. Navy.)

Shown here is another view of a LeTourneau crane and a tractor at work at ATB-Ft. Pierce; however, this time they are pulling the large LCM onto the beach. (Courtesy of the U.S. Navy.)

Here, a Jeheemy crane is maneuvered into position to pick up a landing craft wreck being used as a training aid for landing craft salvage crews. All such men were trained as Jeheemy and LeTourneau crane operators as well as caterpillar tractor drivers. (Courtesy of the U.S. Navy.)

This photograph offers a closer view of a salvage crew training on a Jeheemy crane. Once the ropes and hooks were secure, the wreck would be lifted and rolled away on the crane's tires. (Courtesy of the U.S. Navy.)

Mission accomplished as the Jeheemy crane is ready to roll to the landing craft repair shop. This scene occurred on the Atlantic side of Hutchinson Island. (Courtesy of the U.S. Navy.)

An officer/instructor of the Landing Craft Salvage School gives a dockside lecture on a portable pump used to save swamped landing craft. (Courtesy of the U.S. Navy.)

Salvage crews were trained in making the repairs necessary to keep small landing craft operational. This photograph shows arc welding equipment being used to refurbish a LCM's rudder and propeller. (Courtesy of the U.S. Navy.)

Each landing craft salvage crew had two shipfitters assigned to it, and their mission was working with sheet metal to make structural repairs. Here, shipfitters receive a course in spot welding. (Courtesy of the U.S. Navy.)

Skills such as those learned at ATB-Ft. Pierce would later be used by veterans to help build post-war Florida (and the rest of the United States) and to launch a new era in American history. (Courtesy of the U.S. Navy.)

110,000 MEN HAVE BEEN PROCESSED THROUGH THE U. S. NAVAL BASE HERE

Approximately 110,000 men have been processed in the death-defying practices of beach storming at the United States Naval Amphibious Training base here since its inauguration Jan. 26, 1943.

These figures were announced for the first time today by Captain C. Gulbranson, USN, commanding officer, who also revealed that some 25,000 Army men, as well as hundreds of Marines and Coast Guardsmen, worked with the Navy personnel in the rugged training program that paid dividends on nearly every beachhead the Allies grabbed from the enemy.

At the height of the training period at the local installation, 18,000 men were stationed on the well-guarded oceanfront camp, Captain Gulbranson declared. There are about 5,000 men still a the base.

"It was a revelation to all Nava and military observers to see th Navy and Army personnel wor so harmoniously together," Capt Gulbranson said.

The commanding officer reveale that men were trained at the loca base for an average of $110 pe graduate as compared with $1,00 per man at the next most economy-minded base.

He also expressed pride in th fact that despite the large number of men stationed in this are in the nearly three years th USNATB has operated, there hav been no "bad incidents" created b the personnel of the base. That the captain admits, is a record o which few bases can boast.

This story appeared in the *Fort Pierce News-Tribune* on August 24, 1945, after victory had been achieved in WW II. ATB-Ft. Pierce played a major role in that victory, though in less than a year, the decommissioned base would all but disappear from Ft. Pierce's shores. However, neither Ft. Pierce nor the state of Florida would ever be the same after their experiences during the Second World War.

Select Bibliography

Adams, Larry. "Fiftieth Anniversary Remembrance of the U.S. Naval Amphibious Training Base, Ft. Pierce, Florida Founded in 1943." Ft. Pierce, FL: St. Lucie Historical Society, 1993.

Dwyer, John B. *Scouts and Raiders: The Navy's First Special Warfare Commandos*. Westport, CT: Praeger, 1993.

Fane, Francis D. and Don Moore. *The Naked Warriors: The Story of the U.S. Navy's Frogmen*. New York, 1956, reprint edition. Annapolis: Naval Institute Press, 1995.

Gannon, Michael, ed. *The New History of Florida*. Gainesville: University of Florida Press, 1996.

Lorelli, John A. *To Foreign Shores: U.S. Amphibious Operations in World War II*. Annapolis, MD: Naval Institute Press, 1995.

Rights, Lucille R. *A Portrait of St. Lucie County, Florida*. Virginia Beach, VA: Donning Co., 1994.

Strahan, Jerry E. *Andrew Jackson Higgins and the Boats That Won World War II*. Baton Rouge, LA: Louisiana State University Press, 1994.

Taylor, Robert A. "The Frogmen in Florida: U.S. Navy Combat Demolition Training in Ft. Pierce, 1943–1946." *Florida Historical Quarterly* 75, no. 3 (winter 1997): 289-302.

Witter, Robert E. *Small Boats and Large Slow Targets: Oral Histories of United States Amphibious Forces in WW II*. Missoula, MT: Pictorial Pictures Publishing, 1998.

Wynne, Lewis N., ed. *Florida at War*. St. Leo: St. Leo College Press, 1993.